D1221373

Grasslands

by Delia Goetz

illustrated by Louis Darling

WILLIAM MORROW AND COMPANY   1959

The author wishes to thank Katheryne Thomas Whittemore, Professor of Geography, State University of New York College for Teachers, Buffalo, N. Y., for checking the manuscript.

Grasses are more important to us than any other plants. We depend upon them for green lawns and beautiful parks. Grasses help to prevent floods, they protect our water supply, and they enrich the soil. They furnish much of our food and provide food for the animals whose flesh we eat. Corn, wheat, rice, and sugar cane, for example, are all grasses. Tall, feathery bamboos are grasses, and so are many more plants that furnish products we use every day. Of all plant families, grasses are the largest.

Grasses cover a fifth of the earth's land surface. These areas are the grasslands, where grass is the natural vegetation. Grasslands lie between the moist forest lands and the dry deserts. They are not as dry as deserts, but they do not have sufficient moisture for trees to grow.

Grasses can live under conditions in which most plants cannot survive. They can endure both heat and cold. They thrive where there is little moisture, as well as where there is much. They live in poor soil. Grasses can survive fires that kill tree seedlings, and they

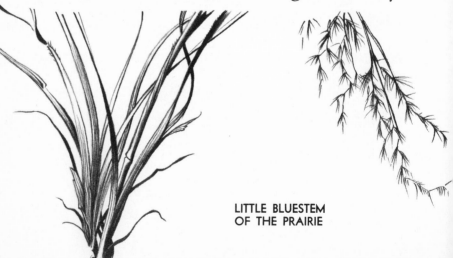

LITTLE BLUESTEM
OF THE PRAIRIE

BUFFALO GRASS OF
THE GREAT PLAINS

can withstand strong winds. All grasses cannot live everywhere. But in such a large family, there are grasses that can live under any of these conditions.

Another reason why grasses are so widespread is that they produce many seeds. Winds and animals and men carry the seeds far and wide. Streams carry seeds far from the plants which produced them. Some seeds are so shaped that they can catch rides. The barbed spines and sharp points of Spanish needles and sandburs cling to the fur or wool of animals and to man's clothing.

Grasslands that cover so much of the earth's surface form three main groups: prairies, steppes, and savannas. Man has made changes on some part of all of them. Great herds of wild animals once roamed the grasslands, but many have disappeared. On other grasslands

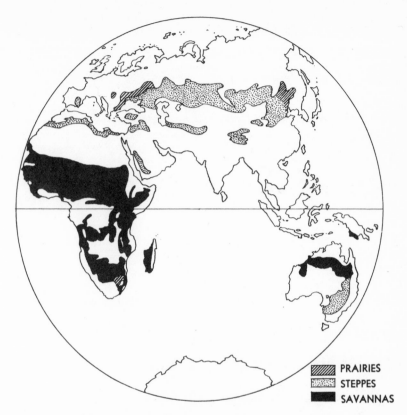

PRAIRIES
STEPPES
SAVANNAS

large herds of domestic animals now graze.
Domestic plants have taken the place of wild
grasses in many areas, because of changes
brought about by man. Nowhere have these
changes been so great as on the prairies, the
lands of tall grass.

PRAIRIES

Prairies are mainly in North and South America, and in European Russia. Lesser prairies are in Africa and Asia.

Wherever they are, prairies are alike in many ways. They are not as dry as the steppes and not as moist as the savannas. Usually they border the edge of a steppe. Prairie soil is dark and deep and fertile. For this reason men could change them from lands that grew only grass to the rich agricultural heart of a nation.

The story of the North American prairie is similar to that of other prairie lands.

White men moving westward came upon the prairie in the middle of North America. From Texas it stretched north to Canada, and from the forest lands of the East to the Great Plains of the West. These Great Plains are semiarid lands where the grass is short, unlike the tall grass of the prairies. Here and there trees and shrubs grew along the prairie rivers or streams. But mostly the prairies were treeless plains stretching to the horizon.

Men who had lived where there were woodlands feared these vast, empty lands. At first they believed that where no trees grew the soil could not be fertile, that there would be no game, that no wood for houses and fuel for fires could be found. But then as the East became crowded, the trek into the vast open prairie began.

Covered wagons were packed with food and clothes, pots and pans, and a few favorite pieces of furniture. Good-by's were said, children were tucked into the wagon, and the parents climbed onto the front seat. "Fall in!" shouted the leader of the wagon train. Whips cracked, hands waved, and one after another the wagons moved toward the great open spaces.

Weeks passed. The long line of wagons moved slowly westward. At last one family after another found the spot where they wished to make a new home.

Soon they learned that many of the tales they had heard were true. Summer winds blew fiercely, baking the soil, drying moisture, and withering the crops. In winter blizzards lashed the prairie. Fires that swept over the land were a constant threat. Even worse was the fear of Indians, and the unwelcome visits of howling wolves and hungry bears.

Here on the prairie men from the East had
to learn new ways of farming. Soil and seasons
differed from those they had known. Their
plows could not turn the tough prairie sod.
Plants that had flourished in their old homes
were choked out by the tall grass. Water was

scarce, and wells had to be dug deeper than in lands of more moisture. There were no fences, and cattle strayed away and were lost. On the vast open plain with few landmarks, even the settlers sometimes lost their way.

QUAIL (BOBWHITE)

PRAIRIE CHICKEN

Despite the hardships, there was much to delight the prairie settlers. Men who had feared there would be no game soon found plenty. Flocks of prairie chickens, wild turkeys, plump partridges, and grouse lived in the tall grass. Deer and bison and rabbits provided meat for many meals. Fish was plentiful in the streams.

Many other living things had their homes
in the grass. Meadow larks teetered on tall
stems to sing their evening songs. Robins and
song sparrows added cheery greetings, and bob-
whites called from the grass.

WILD TURKEY

The first warm spring rains brought a new
growth of grass and with it a host of bright
blossoms. Earliest were the purple-blue pasque
flowers, and soon dogtooth violets nodded on
long slender stems. Golden dandelions, purple
violets, and shooting stars appeared among

the grasses. By midsummer, black-eyed Susans, wild larkspurs, lovely cupped pentstemon, and tall sunflowers were in bloom. Grasses too were in bloom. Spikes of wild rye, gramma grass, bluestem, and needle grass swayed on tall stalks.

Gradually more people settled on the prairies. Neighbors might be miles apart, but still their presence made the prairies seem less lonely. Finally new inventions helped solve some of the prairie farmer's problems. Drills dug deep for wells. Windmills to pump water were fine things on the wind-swept land.

Strong steel plows cut through the tough sod. Machines to plant seeds, reapers, and binders helped lighten the work of the harvest. Meanwhile in Connecticut, a man experimented with a fence to protect his wife's flower garden. The result was barbed wire, an effective means of keeping cattle from straying on the prairie.

Then one day a locomotive whistle broke the stillness of the prairie. Black clouds of smoke billowed, and the first train chugged across the land. Trains brought lumber for new homes, supplies for farm and family, mail from friends far away. Now crops and cattle could be taken quickly to market.

Meanwhile prairie lands were plowed, and tall grass was replaced by other members of the grass family. Miles of corn covered the level prairie. A sea of golden wheat and other grains glowed under the warm sun. Beyond them were lovely summer meadows and lush green pastures.

Many other changes had come to the prairie. Villages with a few stores and a grain elevator near the railroad station grew into large towns and cities. Tiny one-room schools were enlarged. Saplings, planted for protection against the burning sun and fierce winter winds, grew into groves. Orchards hung heavy with fruit. Now the once lonely prairie had become the rich, busy heart of a nation.

The story of the North American prairie is repeated in other parts of the world. The pampas—vast prairie lands of South America—were once lonely. As far as one could see there was only tall grass and blue sky. The squat *ombu* was the only tree native to the pampas. Its gnarled roots grew above the ground and on them the weary traveler sat to rest in the shade.

Hard-riding gauchos—cowboys of the pampas—kept watch over enormous herds of cattle. The rhea bird's sad notes re-echoed the lonely songs the gauchos sang as they rode back and forth. At night their campfires made pinpoints of light on the vast, dark pampas.

When animals were slaughtered for their hides, the meat was left on the plains. There was no practical way of shipping it to a market.

Then men and their inventions changed the pampas as they had the prairie. Steel plows turned the sod, seeds dropped from mechanical planters flourished in the deep, rich soil. When harvest time came, machines helped reap the bountiful crops, and railroads carried them to cities and seaports. Wells and windmills supplied water. Barbed-wire fences enclosed fields and pastures, and the gauchos went to work on the haciendas—the huge ranches of the pampas. Refrigerator cars and ships made it possible to ship meat from the pampas.

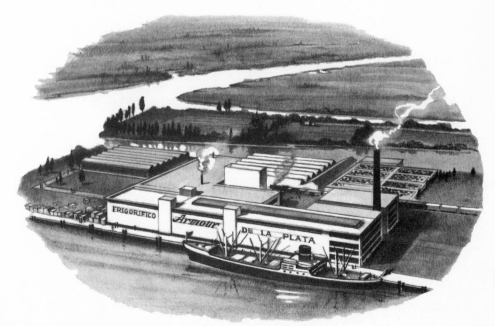

Today vast fields of corn grow on the pampas. Fields of blue-flowered flax reflect the color of the sky, and miles of tall sunflowers turn toward the sun. Forming a great crescent around them are fields of wheat, for the pampas are now the breadbasket of Argentina. Grass still covers part of the pampas and fine cattle are raised there. At the annual stock show in Buenos Aires, proud hacienda owners watch judges pin blue ribbons on their prize-winning animals.

Away from fields and pastures, in well-kept grounds, stands the great house of the hacienda owner. Nearby is the house of the manager and beyond is the cluster of houses where the ranch hands live. Scattered over the hacienda are the houses of the tenant farmers who cultivate some of the land.

Now and then owner and workmen turn out for good times. Slabs of beef brown over the barbecue, and yerba maté, a favorite tea of the pampas, brews over the fire. After the food there is fun — horse races, contests for swinging lassoes called *bolas,* and usually an exciting game of *pato,* which is something like polo.

Changes as great as those on the American prairies have come to the prairie lands in Russia — in the great black earth belt of the Ukraine. Similar in climate to the prairies and pampas, they have the same deep, black soil and similar plants. Vast fields of wheat, corn, and flax, and miles of tall sunflowers make it the rich agricultural land of the country.

STEPPES

The steppes are short-grass lands. They cover more of the earth's surface than any other grasslands. The principal steppes of the world lie on the high plains of southeastern Europe and west central Asia. In North America the Great Plains west of the prairies are steppes. Other steppes cover parts of Australia, Africa, and South America.

Wherever they are, steppes are semiarid. This does not mean half dry and half wet. One year may be dry, another wet. In still another year rains may fall at the wrong time to nourish plants.

Steppes are lands of quick change. In the morning there may be a soft breeze. By afternoon it may become a raging storm, blowing dust or snow, blinding men and animals.

Rains may be gentle drizzles or cloudbursts that flood the dry lands, carrying along rocks and great boulders that gash deep canyons in the earth.

The steppe is a harsh land where men, animals, and plants must adapt themselves to conditions. But on most of the world's steppes, as on the prairies, men have made many changes. Of the large grass family, only those that withstand strong wind, extremes of heat or cold, and lack of moisture can live on the steppe. Many of the plants are a stunted vari-

PRAIRIE DOG

BLACK-FOOTED FERRET

JACK RABBIT

BADGER

ety of the grasses that grow tall on the prairie.

Animals on the steppe must also be able to adapt to life there. They must be able to live on little moisture and food, and at times to do without both. To defend themselves, they must be swift runners or strong fighters. Some must be able to burrow quickly into the dry earth.

No animal on the Great Plains of North America was better equipped to live there than the bison. Like a gigantic, dark, moving carpet, the bison roamed in herds over the grasslands. These huge animals had great strength and endurance. They could live on scant food and water, and go a long time without either. They could withstand great cold and heat, and take care of themselves in blizzards. This they did by facing into the storm instead of drifting with it as cattle or sheep might do.

Good eyesight and keen hearing that warn when danger is near help animals such as the American antelope and the jack rabbit. Its strong limbs enable the antelope to outstrip any wild animal on the American continent. The jack rabbit's legs also help it survive. Prairie dogs, pack rats, and other rodents live well on the dry steppe. Lack of moisture bothers them little, for they produce their own within their bodies.

ANTELOPE (PRONGHORN)

Yet however strong or swift the animal, it could not defend itself against guns. Hunters came to the Great Plains hoping to make their fortunes in hides. They shot bison, took the hide, and left the meat on the plains. Others shot bison and antelope for sport as well as for food. The great herds dwindled until only a few animals are left on the Great Plains.

Men were as destructive of grass as they were of animals. Looking out over the land they saw mile upon mile of grass. And so they increased the size of their herds and grazed them where grass was best. Where land was drier and grass shorter, their flocks of sheep nibbled the grass down to the roots. All year long the great herds grazed the same lands.

The Indians had always moved their flocks back and forth over the plains as seasons changed. In the summer they drove them to

the mountain pastures. When cold winter winds blew, they turned them toward the lowlands. In dry climates, grass grows slowly. They knew they must give it time to grow.

But the white men continued to graze their flocks on the same lands. Patches of bare soil appeared between the grass plants. More grass was eaten to the roots and died, and the bare spots grew larger. Weeds replaced the grass. Wind blew soil where roots no longer held it.

Even more destructive of the grassland than the cattlemen who overgrazed it were the farmers. They came with dreams of turning the plains into rich farms such as they saw on the prairie. They too failed to adapt their ways to the steppe. Grassland was plowed and crops that had flourished on the moist prairie were planted.

When rains fell, crops grew and men prospered. But these are semiarid lands. There were years when little rain fell. Dry, hot winds blew over the fields and crops withered and died. Even more discouraging were the years when fine crops were mowed down by hordes of grasshoppers and locusts. Loose soil drifted like snow on the fields. Wind lifted tons of soil from one man's farm and dropped it on his neighbor's. Rain washed deep gullies in the topsoil.

Many families deserted their farms. Others stayed but adapted their ways to the land in which they lived. Cattlemen no longer let their animals graze all the year in the same place, but moved them from one pasture to another to give the grass time to grow. Some fenced their fields and planted some to grain, leaving the rest to grass.

Now they used methods of cultivation better suited to the steppe. Where there was water, fields and pastures were irrigated. Cattle that thrived on dry lands of other countries were imported. Some places that had been overgrazed were seeded with grass.

The loneliest steppe in the world is in Outer Mongolia in the heart of Asia. There people depend on their flocks for food and for warm woolen clothes. They live in round tents, called yurts. These have a framework of wood covered with thick felt made with wool from their flocks.

Like most nomads, the Mongol herdsmen are hospitable people, happy to share food and shelter with their guests. In summer they drive herds of cows, camels, yaks, goats, and horses to graze on the high plains. When cold winds blow over the high pastures, they bring them to lower ground.

Modern ways are catching up with the Mongols in their isolated grasslands. Homes of stone and brick are replacing the yurts. Western clothes are becoming popular. Young men are studying to be engineers and doctors and teachers. Yet in isolated corners of the steppes, nomads cling to century-old ways of life.

Many of Russia's once parched steppes are irrigated now. Here grow vast fields of cotton, wheat, and other grains. Nomads have settled on the land, and villages have grown into prosperous cities.

Australia's steppe is still sparsely settled. But the radio programs beamed to these people help keep them in touch with the rest of the country. Radio is also bringing lessons to their children who have no schools.

And so the world's steppes are changing, but they are still the grazing lands for animals and a source of food and other products for man.

SAVANNAS

Savannas are the large tropical grasslands that lie in Africa and the interior of Brazil. Smaller savannas cover some parts of all the continents. Coarse grasses with sharp, saw-toothed edges usually grow in savannas. The stunted trees and shrubs scattered through the savannas give them a different appearance from other grasslands. The rounded tops of acacias, like open umbrellas, are a familiar sight in most savannas. Tall eucalyptus, palms, pines, juniper, and yucca also grow in many of them.

Plentiful rain falls on the savannas part of the year. With the first showers, grasses begin to grow and trees leaf out. Plants grow quickly in the tropical heat and moisture. Near the moist forests savanna grass grows very tall, but toward the desert the grass is short and sparse. In the rainy season streams and rivers overflow and flood the land.

After a few months rains slacken, then stop. Waters of the rivers recede and streams dwindle and dry up. Mud dries and cracks. Trees drop their leaves and grasses turn yellow and brown. Hot winds rustle the tall, dry stalks. Plants drop their seeds and die, and only the roots of others are alive. Animals search the savannas for water, and herders drive their cattle from one water hole to another.

With the dry season comes the danger of fire. Here on the savannas it is as much feared as it once was on the prairies. Herdsmen sometimes burn off the old grass, and the fire left unguarded quickly turns the savanna into an ocean of flame. Young trees are burned to the ground and the roots are killed.

Animals well known in our zoos make their home in the savannas of Africa. Fleet-footed gazelles speed through the tall grass past clumsy wild hogs. The bold stripes of the timid zebras blend with the shadows in the green vegetation. The bad-tempered rhinoceros makes its home there, and herds of elephants go on their way without fear of enemies. Tall giraffes nibble the tops of acacia trees. All of these animals are grass eaters.

CHEETAH

Other animals invade the savannas to feed on the grass eaters. Leopards lie on low branches or steal through the tall grass to pounce on a helpless zebra or gazelle. The fierce cheetah looks for easy prey. At night the cowardly hyena's powerful jaws snap shut on its victims. And in the tall grass near water holes lions lie in wait to seize animals who come to drink.

These fierce animals are not the only hunters in the savannas. For years big-game hunters have come there to kill for sport. Gradually, in parts of the savannas, as in the prairies and steppes, some animals are becoming scarce.

Insects, the real pests of these tropical grass-lands, are still numerous there. Most feared are the mosquitoes, ticks, and tsetse fly. These blood-sucking insects carry germs of deadly diseases from men and animals and infect others. Slowly campaigns to control the spread of diseases caused by insects are bringing results.

People also live in Africa's savannas. Like people of other grasslands, they have different customs. The proud Masai are cattlemen. They raise their long-horned herds near the big-game country of eastern Africa. The Masai are fierce warriors and are proud of the fact that they have never been slaves. They fear neither

man nor beast, and a Masai will boldly attack a lion that dares to molest his herd.

Masai are as vain of their dress as they are proud of their strength. Both men and women dress in garments of leather or of brilliantly colored cloth. The women are fond of elaborate decorations, especially the metal spirals that reach from wrist to elbow and from ankle to knee.

The Hausas who live in the savannas of eastern Africa are also fond of elaborate decorations. Of iron and tin they make attractive necklaces, pins, and bracelets. They also turn out fine scissors, swords, and daggers. Hausas are good.farmers as well as fine craftsmen. They wisely suit crops and methods of cultiva-

YOUNG COFFEE BUSHES

tion to the seasons. They rotate their crops and cultivate the soil so that it holds moisture during the dry season.

Large coffee plantations have replaced much of Brazil's savannas. But vast herds of cattle still graze on the *llanos,* the savannas of Venezuela.

The face of the grasslands has changed over the years. But the crops that replace the natural vegetation have not changed man's need for grasslands. How best to preserve and improve them is a problem which should concern all of us.